Also by Jack Gilbert

Views of Jeopardy
Monolithos
The Great Fires
Refusing Heaven

Tough Heaven
Poems of Pittsburgh

Tough Heaven
Poems of Pittsburgh

Jack Gilbert

Pond Road Press
North Truro, Massachusetts
Washington, D.C.

Copyright © 2006 by Jack Gilbert

All rights reserved under International and Pan American Copyright Convention.
Published in the United States of America by arrangement with Alfred A. Knopf,
a division of Random House, Inc.:
From *Monolithos:* (1982) "The Whiteness, the Sound and Alcibiades,"
and "Who's There."

All rights reserved under International and Pan American Copyright Convention.
Published in the United States of America by arrangement with Alfred A. Knopf,
a division of Random House, Inc.:
From *The Great Fires:* (1994) "Measuring the Tyger," "Voices Inside and Out," "Tear
It Down," "Searching for Pittsburgh," "Steel Guitars," "The Spirit and the Soul,"
"Ruins and Wabi," "Trying to Have Something Left Over,"
"Carrying Torches at Noon," and "Chastity."

All rights reserved under International and Pan American Copyright Convention.
Published in the United States of America by arrangement with Alfred A. Knopf,
a division of Random House, Inc.:
From *Refusing Heaven*: (2005) "What Song Should We Sing," "Elegy for Bob,"
"Getting Away with It," "Refusing Heaven," "A Thanksgiving Dance," "Looking at
Pittsburgh from Paris," "The Lost World," and "A Taste for Grit and Whatever."

Further acknowledgments follow page 24.

ISBN: 0-9719741-3-6

First Pond Road Press Printing (Limited Edition) 2006
Pond Road Press, established in 2003 by Mary Ann Larkin and Patric Pepper,
publishes literary chapbooks.

Cover photo by Holmes I. Mettee
Carnegie Museum of Art, Pittsburgh; Gift of N. Boyd Mettee

Online and mail orders:
Pond Road Press
221 Channing Street NE
Washington, DC 20002-1025
pepperlarkin@juno.com
www.pondroadpress.com,
or from
Amazon.com

for Gerald Stern and Jean McLean

It was Pittsburgh that lasted.

Contents

Foreword

Chastity	3
Elegy for Bob	4
Searching for Pittsburgh	5
A Taste for Grit and Whatever	6
Voices Inside and Out	7
The Whiteness, the Sound, and Alcibiades	8
Carrying Torches at Noon	10
Tear It Down	11
Trying to Have Something Left Over	12
Refusing Heaven	13
Measuring the Tyger	14
What Song Should We Sing	15
Steel Guitars	16
The Spirit and the Soul	17
Looking at Pittsburgh from Paris	19
Getting Away with It	20
Ruins and Wabi	21
Who's There	22
A Thanksgiving Dance	23
The Lost World	24

Foreword

Jack Gilbert left Pittsburgh as a young man but "Pittsburgh is still tangled in him," he tells us as he approaches eighty years of age. He needs the mills "even though they are gone, to measure against." He knows luxury by the sound of the trees that filled his childhood. He builds his Pittsburgh again and again:

> In Paris afternoons on Buttes-Chaumont. On Greek islands
> with their fields of stone. In beds with women, sometimes,
> amid their gentleness....

In these poems, we see Gilbert using the brutality and beauty of Pittsburgh, its sights and sounds and smells, to make himself into the man and artist he wants to be. In the process, he not only describes the city of his youth—"...brick and tired wood. Ox and sovereign spirit"—but takes the brawling Pittsburgh of rivers, streetcars and railroads, bridges and mills, and transmutes it into "the mind's steel / and the riveted girders of the soul," even into himself in old age: "A cauldron of cooling melt." Here, the physical becomes the spiritual. The language of steel describes the making of the poet:

> The weight of the mind fractures
> the girders and piers of the spirit, spilling out
> the heart's melt....

Even as a boy, brooding on carnival women:

> He vaguely understood that it was not
> their flesh that was a mystery but something on the other
> side of it....

Gilbert takes from the city of his birth and young manhood, Pittsburgh's lushness and severity, its irresistible power, and forges them into the "tough heaven" of these poems.

Mary Ann Connors Larkin

Tough Heaven
Poems of Pittsburgh

CHASTITY

A boy sits on the porch of a wooden house,
reading *War and Peace*.
Down below, it is Sunday afternoon in August.
The street is deserted except
for the powerful sun. There is a sound,
and he looks. At the bottom of the long
flight of steps, a man has fallen.
The boy gets up, not wanting to.
All year he has thought about honesty,
and he sits down. Two people finally come
and call the ambulance.
But too late. When everybody is gone,
he reads some pages, and stops.
Sits a moment, turns back to the place,
and starts again.

Elegy for Bob (Jean McLean)

Only you and I still stand in the snow on Highland Avenue
in Pittsburgh waiting for the blundering iron streetcars
that never came. Only you know how the immense storms
over the Allegheny and Monongahela rivers were the scale
I wanted. Nobody but you remembers Peabody High School.
You shared my youth in Paris and the hills above Como.
And later, in Seattle. It was you playing the aria from
Don Giovanni over and over, filling the forest of Puget
Sound with the music. You in the front room and me
upstairs with your discarded wife in my bed. The sound
of your loneliness pouring over our happy bodies.
You were with your third wife when I was in Perugia
six months later, but were in love with somebody else.
We searched for her in Munich, the snow falling again.
You trying to decide when to kill yourself. All of it
finally bringing us to San Francisco. To the vast
decaying white house. No sound of Mozart coming up
from there. No alleluias in you anymore. No longer
will you waltz under the chandeliers in Paris salons
drunk with champagne and the Greek girl as the others
stand along the mirrored walls. The men watching
with fury, the eyes of the women inscrutable. No one
else speaks the language of those years. No one
remembers you as the Baron. The streetcars have
finished the last run, and I am walking home. Thinking
love is not refuted because it comes to an end.

SEARCHING FOR PITTSBURGH

The fox pushes softly, blindly through me at night,
between the liver and the stomach. Comes to the heart
and hesitates. Considers and then goes around it.
Trying to escape the mildness of our violent world.
Goes deeper, searching for what remains of Pittsburgh
in me. The rusting mills sprawled gigantically
along three rivers. The authority of them.
The gritty alleys where we played every evening were
stained pink by the inferno always surging in the sky,
as though Christ and the Father were still fashioning
the Earth. Locomotives driving through the cold rain,
lordly and bestial in their strength. Massive water
flowing morning and night throughout a city
girded with ninety bridges. Sumptuous-shouldered,
sleek-thighed, obstinate and majestic, unquenchable.
All grip and flood, mighty sucking and deep-rooted grace.
A city of brick and tired wood. Ox and sovereign spirit.
Primitive Pittsburgh. Winter month after month telling
of death. The beauty forcing us as much as harshness.
Our spirits forged in that wilderness, our minds forged
by the heart. Making together a consequence of America.
The fox watched me build my Pittsburgh again and again.
In Paris afternoons on Buttes-Chaumont. On Greek islands
with their fields of stone. In beds with women, sometimes,
amid their gentleness. Now the fox will live in our ruined
house. My tomatoes grow ripe among weeds and the sound
of water. In this happy place my serious heart has made.

A Taste for Grit and Whatever

More and more it is the incidental that makes
him yearn, and he worries about that.
Why should the single railroad tracks
curving away into the bare December trees
and no houses matter? And why is it
the defeated he trusts? Is it because
Pittsburgh is still tangled in him that he
has the picture on his wall of God's head
torn apart by jungle roots? Maybe
growing up in that brutal city left him
with a taste for grit and whatever it was
he saw in the titanic rusting steel mills.
It might be the reason he finally moved out
of Paris. Perhaps it is the scale
of those long ago winters that makes him
restless when people laugh a lot.
Why the erotic matters so much. Not as
pleasure but a way to get to something darker.
Hunting down the soul, searching out the iron
of Heaven when the work is getting done.

VOICES INSIDE AND OUT

>for Hayden Carruth

When I was a child, there was an old man with
a ruined horse who drove his wagon through the back
streets of our neighborhood, crying, *Iron! Iron!*
Meaning he would buy bedsprings and dead stoves.
Meaning for me, in the years since, the mind's steel
and the riveted girders of the soul. When I lived
on Ile Saint-Louis, a glazier came every morning,
crying *Vitre! Vitre!* Meaning the glass on his back,
but sounding like the swallows swooping years later
at evening outside my high windows in Perugia.
In my boyhood summers, Italian men came walking ahead
of the truck calling out the ripeness of their melons,
and old Jews slogged in the snow, crying, *Brooms! Brooms!*
Two hundred years ago, the London shop boys yelled
at people going by, *What do you lack?* A terrible
question to hear every day. "Less and less," I think.
The Brazilians say, "In this country we have everything
we need, except what we don't have."

The Whiteness, the Sound, and Alcibiades

So I come on this birthday at last
here in the house of strangers.
With a broken pair of shoes,
no profession, and a few poems.
After all that promise.
Not by addiction or play, by choices.
By concern for whales and love,
for elephants and Alcibiades.
But to arrive at so little product.
A few corners done,
an arcade up but unfaced,
and everywhere the ambitious
unfinished monuments to Myshkin
and magnitude. Like persisting
on the arrogant steeple of Beauvais.

I wake in Trastevere
in the house of city-peasants,
and lie in the noise dreaming
of the wealth of summer nights
from my childhood when the dark
was sixty feet deep in luxury,
of elm and maple and sycamore.
I wandered hour by hour
with my gentle, bewildered need,
following the faint sound
of women in the moving leaves.

In Latium, years ago,
I sat by the road watching
an ox come through the day.
Stark-white in the distance.

Occasionally under a tree.
Colorless in the heavy sun.
Suave in the bright shadows.
Starch-white near in the glare.
Petal-white near in the shade.
Linen, stone-white, and milk.
Ox-white before me, and past
into the thunder of light.

For ten years I have tried
to understand about the ox.
About the sound. The whales.
Of love. And arrived here
to give thanks for the profit.
I wake to the wanton freshness.
To the arriving and leaving. To the journey.
I wake to the freshness. And do reverence.

Carrying Torches at Noon

The boy came home from school and found a hundred lamps
filling the house. Lamps everywhere and all turned on
despite the summer shining in the handsome windows.
Two and three lamps on every table. Lamps in chairs
and on the rugs and even in the kitchen. More lamps
upstairs and on the topmost floor as well. All brightly
burning, until the police came and took them away.
An excess of light that continued in him for a long time.
The radiance of lamps flourishing in the day became
a benchmark for his heart, became a Beaufort scale
for his appetites. The wildness and gladness of it,
the illicitness in him magnified the careful gleam
of Paris mornings when he got to them, and the dark
glisten of the Seine each night as he crossed
the stone bridges back to his room. It was the same
years later as the snow fell through the bruised light
of a winter afternoon and he stood in a narrow street
telling Anna he was leaving. All of it a light beyond
anybody's ability to manage. The Massachusetts sunlight
lies comfortably on the maples. The Pittsburgh lamps
inside of him make it look maybe not good enough.

Tear It Down

We find out the heart only by dismantling what
the heart knows. By redefining the morning,
we find a morning that comes just after darkness.
We can break through marriage into marriage.
By insisting on love we spoil it, get beyond
affection and wade mouth-deep into love.
We must unlearn the constellations to see the stars.
But going back toward childhood will not help.
The village is not better than Pittsburgh.
Only Pittsburgh is more than Pittsburgh.
Rome is better than Rome in the same way the sound
of raccoon tongues licking the inside walls
of the garbage tub is more than the stir
of them in the muck of the garbage. Love is not
enough. We die and are put into the earth forever.
We should insist while there is still time. We must
eat through the wildness of her sweet body already
in our bed to reach the body within that body.

Trying to Have Something Left Over

There was a great tenderness to the sadness
when I would go there. She knew how much
I loved my wife and that we had no future.
We were like casualties helping each other
as we waited for the end. Now I wonder
if we understood how happy those Danish
afternoons were. Most of the time we did not talk.
Often I took care of the baby while she did
housework. Changing him and making him laugh.
I would say *Pittsburgh* softly each time before
throwing him up. Whisper *Pittsburgh* with
my mouth against the tiny ear and throw
him higher. Pittsburgh and happiness high up.
The only way to leave even the smallest trace.
So that all his life her son would feel gladness
unaccountably when anyone spoke of the ruined
city of steel in America. Each time almost
remembering something maybe important that got lost.

REFUSING HEAVEN

The old women in black at early Mass in winter
are a problem for him. He could tell by their eyes
they have seen Christ. They make the kernel
of his being and the clarity around it
seem meager, as though he needs girders
to hold up his unusable soul. But he chooses
against the Lord. He will not abandon his life.
Not his childhood, not the ninety-two bridges
across the two rivers of his youth. Nor the mills
along the banks where he became a young man
as he worked. The mills are eaten away, and eaten
again by the sun and its rusting. He needs them
even though they are gone, to measure against.
The silver is worn down to the brass underneath
and is the better for it. He will gauge
by the smell of concrete sidewalks after night rain.
He is like an old ferry dragged on to the shore,
a home in its smashed grandeur, with the giant beams
and joists. Like a wooden ocean out of control.
A beached heart. A cauldron of cooling melt.

Measuring the Tyger

Barrels of chains. Sides of beef stacked in vans.
Water buffalo dragging logs of teak in the river mud
outside Mandalay. Pantocrater in the Byzantium dome.
The mammoth overhead crane bringing slabs of steel
through the dingy light and roar to the giant shear
that cuts the adamantine three-quarter-inch plates
and they flop down. The weight of the mind fractures
the girders and piers of the spirit, spilling out
the heart's melt. Incandescent ingots big as cars
trundling out of titanic mills, red slag scaling off
the brighter metal in the dark. The Monongahela River
below, night's sheen on its belly. Silence except
for the machinery clanging deeper in us. You will
love again, people say. Give it time. Me with time
running out. Day after day of the everyday.
What they call real life, made of eighth-inch gauge.
Newness strutting around as if it were significant.
Irony, neatness and rhyme pretending to be poetry.
I want to go back to that time after Michiko's death
when I cried every day among the trees. To the real.
To the magnitude of pain, of being that much alive.

What Song Should We Sing

The massive overhead crane comes
when we wave to it, lets down
its heavy claws and waits tamely
within its power while we hook up
the slabs of three-quarter-inch
steel. Takes away the ponderous
reality when we wave again.
What name do we have for that?
What song is there for its voice?
What is the other face of Yahweh?
The god who made the slug and ferret,
the maggot and shark in his image.
What is the carol for that?
Is it the song of nevertheless,
or of the empire of our heart? We carry
language as our mind, but are we
the dead whale that sinks grandly
for years to reach the bottom of us?

Steel Guitars

The world is announced by the smell of oregano and sage
in rocky places high up, with white doves higher still
in the blue sky. Or the faint voices of women and girls
in the olive trees below, and a lustrous sea beneath that.
Like thoughts of lingerie while reading *Paradise Lost*
in Alabama. Or the boy in Pittsburgh that only summer
he was nine, prowling near the rusty railroad yard
where they put up vast tents and a man lifted anvils
with chains through his nipples. The boy listened
for the sound that made him shiver as he ran hard
across the new sawdust to see the two women again
on a platform above his head, indolent and almost naked
in the simple daylight. Reality stretched thin
as he watched their painted eyes brooding on what
they contained. He vaguely understood that it was not
their flesh that was a mystery but something on the other
side of it. Now the man remembering the boy knows
there is a door. We go through and hear a sound
like buildings burning, like the sound of a stone hitting
a stone in the dark. The heart in its plenty hammered
by rain and need, by the weight of what momentarily is.

THE SPIRIT AND THE SOUL

It should have been the family that lasted.
Should have been my sister and my peasant mother.
But it was not. They were the affection,
not the journey. It could have been my father,
but he died too soon. Gelmetti and Gregg
and Nogami lasted. It was the newness of me,
and the newness after that, and newness again.
It was the important love and the serious lust.
It was Pittsburgh that lasted. The iron and fog
and sooty brick houses. Not Aunt Mince and Pearl,
but the black-and-white winters with their girth
and geological length of cold. Streets ripped
apart by ice and emerging like wounded beasts when
the snow finally left in April. Freight trains
with their steam locomotives working at night.
Summers the size of crusades. When I was a boy,
I saw downtown a large camera standing in front
of the William Pitt Hotel or pointed at Kaufmann's
Department Store. Usually around midnight,
but the people still going by. The camera set
slow enough that cars and people left no trace.
The crowds in Rome and Tokyo and Manhattan
did not last. But the empty streets of Perugia,
my two bowls of bean soup on Kos, and Pimpaporn
Charionpanith lasted. The plain nakedness of Anna
in Denmark remains in me forever. The wet lilacs
on Highland Avenue when I was fourteen. Carrying
Michiko dead in my arms. It is not about the spirit.
The spirit dances, comes and goes. But the soul
is nailed to us like lentils and fatty bacon lodged
under the ribs. What lasted is what the soul ate.

The way a child knows the world by putting it
part by part into his mouth. As I tried to gnaw
my way into the Lord, working to put my heart
against that heart. Lying in the wheat at night,
letting the rain after all the dry months have me.

Looking at Pittsburgh from Paris

The boat of his heart is tethered to the ancient
stone bridges. Beached on the Pacific hills with
thick evening fog flooding whitely over the ridge.
Running in front of the Provençal summer. Drowned
as a secret under the broad Monongahela River.
Forever richly laden with Oak Street and Umbria.
"There be monsters," they warn in the blank spaces
of the old maps. But the real danger is the ocean's
insufficiency, the senseless repetition throughout
the empty waters. Calm and storms and calm again.
Too impoverished for the human. We come to know
ourselves as immense continents and archipelagoes
of endless bounty. He waits now in the hold
of a wooden ship. Becalmed, maybe standing to.
Bobbing, rocking softly. The cargo of ghosts
and angels all around. The wraiths, surprisingly,
singing with the clear voices of young boys.
The angels clapping the rhythm. As he watches
for morning, for the dark to give way and show
his landfall, the new country, his native land.

Getting Away with It

We have already lived in the real paradise.
Horses in the empty summer street.
Me eating the hot wurst I couldn't afford,
in frozen Munich, tears dropping. We can
remember. A child in the outfield waiting
for the last fly ball of the year. So dark
already it was black against heaven.
The voices trailing away to dinner,
calling faintly in the immense distance.
Standing with my hands open, watching it
curve over and start down, turning white
at the last second. Hands down. Flourishing.

Ruins and Wabi

To tell the truth, Storyville was brutal. The parlors
of even the fancy whorehouses crawling with roaches
and silverfish. The streets foul and the sex brawling.
But in the shabby clapboard buildings on Franklin
and on Liberty and on Iberville was the invention.
Throughout the District, you could hear Tony Jackson
and King Oliver, Morton and Bechet finding it night
after night. Like the dream Bellocq's photographs found
in the midst of Egypt Vanita and Mary Meathouse, Aunt Cora
and Gold Tooth Gussie. It takes a long time to get
the ruins right. The Japanese think it strange we paint
our old wooden houses when it takes so long to find
the *wabi* in them. They prefer the bonsai tree after
the valiant blossoming is over, the leaves fallen. When
bareness reveals a merit born in the vegetable struggling.

Who's There

I hear the trees with surprise after California,
having forgotten the sound that filled my childhood.
I hear the maples and vast elms again. American oak,
English oak, pin oak. Honey locust and mountain ash.
Catalpa, beech, and sycamore. I hear the luxury again
just before autumn. And remember the old riddle:
Winter will take it all, the trees will go on.
This grass will die and this lawn continue. What then
goes on of the child I was? Of that boy taunted
by the lush whispering every summer night in Pittsburgh?
All those I have been are the generalization that tastes
this plum. Brothers who knew all the women I loved.
But did we share or alternate? Was I with Gianna
among the olive trees those evenings in Perugia?
Am I the one who heard with Linda the old Danish men
singing up out of the snow and dark far down below us?

A Thanksgiving Dance

His spirit dances the long ago, and later.
Starlight on a country road in worn-out
western Pennsylvania. The smell of weeds
and rusting iron. And gladness.
His spirit welcomes the Italian New Year's
in a hill town filled with the music
of glass crashing everywhere in the cobbled
streets. Champagne and the first kisses.
Too shy to look at each other and no language
between them. He dances alone, the dance
of after that. Now they sit amid the heavy
Roman sunlight and talk of the people
they are married to now. He secretly
dances the waltz she was in her astonishing
beauty, drinking wine and laughing, the window
behind her filled with winter rain.

The Lost World

Think what it was like, he said. Peggy Lee and Goodman
all the time. Carl Ravazza making me crazy
with "Vieni Su" from a ballroom in New Jersey
every night, the radio filling my dark room
in Pittsburgh with naked-shouldered women
in black gowns. Helen Forest and Helen O'Connell,
and later the young Sarah Vaughan out of Chicago
from midnight until two. Think of being fifteen
in the middle of leafy June when Sinatra and Ray
Eberle both had number-one records of "Fools Rush In."
Somebody singing "Tenderly" and somebody doing
"This Love of Mine." Helplessly adolescent while
the sound of romance was constantly everywhere.
All day long out of windows along the street.
Sinatra with "Close to You." And all the bands. Artie
Shaw with "Green Eyes" and whoever was always playing
"Begin the Beguine." Me desperate because I wouldn't
get there in time. Who can blame me for my heart?
What choice did I have? Harry James with "Sleepy
Lagoon." Imagine, on a summer night, "Sleepy Lagoon"!

ACKNOWLEDGMENTS

The author and publisher wish to thank Henry Lyman for his endlessly generous assistance in preparing this book.

Thanks, too, to Nina Graybill, Tawny Harding, Sam Hazo, Jane and Brockie Stevenson, Helen Wilson, and the reference librarians from the Enoch Pratt Free Library in Baltimore. Gratitude also goes to the staff at Knopf: Deborah Garrison, Thomas Dobrowski and Elizabeth Cochrane.

Particular appreciation goes to Larry Kennedy and his friend John Oyler for their research, which led to Walter Rush, Hazelwood steelworker, identifying the steel works in the Holmes Mettee cover photo.

Jack Gilbert wishes to acknowledge the following publishers of the poems included in this volume:

American Poetry Review: "Tear It Down"

Ploughshares: "Voices Inside and Out"

Poetry East: "Searching for Pittsburgh," and "Steel Guitars"

The New Yorker: "Refusing Heaven"

About Jack Gilbert

JACK GILBERT was born in Pittsburgh in 1925 and grew up in East Liberty. After attending Peabody High School he worked as an exterminator, a door-to-door salesman, and steelworker, eventually graduating from the University of Pittsburgh. He has lived much of his life outside the United States, publishing infrequently. He is the author of *Views of Jeopardy* (1962), winner of the Yale Younger Poets Series; *Monolithos* (1982), a finalist for the Pulitzer Prize; *The Great Fires* (1994); and *Refusing Heaven* (2005), winner of the National Book Critics Circle Award. He was married to the American poet Linda Gregg and the late Japanese poet Michiko Nogami, to whom he dedicated a limited edition of elegaic poems published under the title *Kochan* (1982). He presently lives in Northampton, Massachusetts.

About Jack Gilbert's Poetry

"Gilbert isn't just a remarkable poet. He's a poet whose directness and lucidity ought to appeal to lots of readers.... Indeed, what's powerful about Gilbert is that he is a rarity, especially in this day and age: the poet who stands outside his own time, practicing a poetics of purity in an ever-more cacophonous world.... No other poet I know captures so well a mind torn between the pleasures of austerity and the fecund, intoxicating powers of abundance. What Gilbert is searching for, poem after poem, are the ideal circumstances where the two intersect, and privation becomes a form of richness.... Gilbert's poems about women can, I think, be thought of as still lifes in the manner of visual arts, where we still find such deliberate, rational acts of paying reverence to female beauty acceptable—even expected. These poems are part and parcel of his larger project: rescuing from the debilitating forces of cynicism a conviction that transcendence can await us in this world."

Meghan O'Rourke
Slate

"...Stunning vistas and masterfully crafted works of heartbreaking beauty.... He forges his own path with writing that is at once intellectually dense and profoundly human. His work radiates with humility and awe, and he brings an intellectual heft that is often lacking in contemporary poetry.... Rather than declare answers, he stubbornly asks how to be human in a world of loss, violence, failures and suffering.... Gilbert has often been called a poet of loss but these poems are rich with having— the Mediterranean sun, catching a fly ball, the lessons of solitude."

Elizabeth Hoover
Los Angeles Times

About Holmes I. Mettee

JONES & LAUGHLIN STEEL CORPORATION, Pittsburgh Works at Hazelwood from across the Monongahela River, 1925

METTEE operated from the Holmes I. Mettee Studio, Photographers, in Baltimore from 1924 until his premature death at the age of 62 in 1947. Mettee's amateur photography won him national and international awards including a first prize awarded him by Alfred Stieglitz at the Wanamaker Salon in New York City. His success led him to leave his job as a sales manager to open his own studio, specializing, and gaining world recognition, in industrial photography. Additional Mettee photos of 1925 Pittsburgh were exhibited in 2005 at the Keith de Lellis Gallery in New York City in a show of industrial photography. The Carnegie Museum of Art, Pittsburgh, also owns other Mettee photos of industrial Pittsburgh, donated to the Museum by Mettee's son, N. Boyd Mettee, a noted photographer himself.

About Design and Production

Book design by Mary Ann Larkin and Patric Pepper.
Composition by Patric Pepper.

The text type is Adobe Electra, a typeface designed by W.A. Dwiggins (1880-1956). Electra cannot be classified as either modern or old-style. It is not based on any historical model, nor does it echo a particular period or style. It avoids the extreme contrast between thick and thin elements that marks most modern faces and attempts to give a feeling of fluidity, power, and speed.

The cover type, for both title and text, is Palatino Linotype, first designed by Hermann Zapf in 1950. The font was named after Giambattista Palatino, a master of calligraphy from the time of Leonardo da Vinci. Palatino is a typeface based on classical Italian Renaissance forms, and has become a modern classic in itself for both text and display typography.

Printed on 50% recycled, acid free paper in the United States of America by McNaughton & Gunn, Inc.